EXPLORING VOLCANOES

VOLCANOLOGISTS AT WORK!

ELSIE OLSON

Consulting Editor, Diane Craig, M.A./Reading Specialist

Super Sandcastle

An Imprint of Abdo Publishing
abdopublishing.com

abdopublishing.com

Published by Abdo Publishing, a division of ABDO, PO Box 398166, Minneapolis, Minnesota 55439. Copyright © 2018 by Abdo Consulting Group, Inc. International copyrights reserved in all countries. No part of this book may be reproduced in any form without written permission from the publisher. Super SandCastle™ is a trademark and logo of Abdo Publishing.

Printed in the United States of America, North Mankato, Minnesota

102017
012018

Design: Kelly Doudna, Mighty Media, Inc.
Production: Mighty Media, Inc.
Editor: Jessie Alkire
Cover Photographs: Science Source; Shutterstock
Interior Photographs: iStockphoto; NASA/JPL-CalTech; Science Source; Shutterstock; Wikimedia Commons

Publisher's Cataloging-in-Publication Data

Names: Olson, Elsie, author.
Title: Exploring volcanoes: volcanologists at work! / by Elsie Olson.
Other titles: Volcanologists at work!
Description: Minneapolis, Minnesota : Abdo Publishing, 2018. | Series: Earth detectives |
Identifiers: LCCN 2017946457 | ISBN 9781532112331 (lib.bdg.) | ISBN 9781614799757 (ebook)
Subjects: LCSH: Volcanological research--Juvenile literature. | Earth sciences--Juvenile literature. |
    Occupations--Juvenile literature.
Classification: DDC 551.21--dc23
LC record available at https://lccn.loc.gov/2017946457

Super SandCastle™ books are created by a team of professional educators, reading specialists, and content developers around five essential components—phonemic awareness, phonics, vocabulary, text comprehension, and fluency—to assist young readers as they develop reading skills and strategies and increase their general knowledge. All books are written, reviewed, and leveled for guided reading, early reading intervention, and Accelerated Reader™ programs for use in shared, guided, and independent reading and writing activities to support a balanced approach to literacy instruction.

CONTENTS

WHAT IS A VOLCANO?

A volcano is a vent in Earth's surface. This vent connects to Earth's **molten** interior. Most volcanoes look like mountains.

Sometimes volcanoes erupt. Gas, rocks, or **lava** come out of them. This can happen slowly. It can also happen quickly and make an explosion. This often causes **damage**.

Volcanoes can form islands and mountains.
Volcanic soil is good for growing crops.

WHO STUDIES VOLCANOES?

Some scientists study volcanoes. They are called volcanologists. These scientists explore how volcanoes work. They learn why volcanoes erupt. Then they try to **predict** eruptions.

Eruptions can be deadly. They are hard to predict. But doing so can save lives. It gives people time to **evacuate**.

Volcanologists can study eruptions as they occur. But they also study inactive volcanoes. Some volcanoes haven't erupted for thousands of years!

ANCIENT ERUPTIONS

Humans have lived near volcanoes for thousands of years. In the year 79, Mount Vesuvius erupted. It is in Italy. Many people were killed. Survivors took notes about the event. Scientists still look at their writings today.

Studying volcanoes became an official science in the 1800s. This science is called volcanology.

Mount Vesuvius

Mount Vesuvius destroyed the city of Pompeii, Italy. The ruins still exist today!

MAURICE AND KATIA KRAFFT

Maurice and Katia Krafft were French volcanologists. They studied volcanoes across the world. The Kraffts were often feet away from **lava** flows!

The Kraffts were famous for their eruption photos and videos.

President Corazon Aquino of the Philippines watched the Kraffts' eruption footage. It helped him decide to evacuate thousands of people when Mount Pinatubo erupted in 1991.

LOVING VOLCANOES

The Kraffts dreamed of being volcanologists from a young age. The two met while in college in France. They married in 1970.

The Kraffts spent the next 20 years filming eruptions. They also helped **predict** them. The Kraffts improved **evacuation** methods. This saved many lives.

In 1991, the Kraffts filmed an eruption. They were at Mount Unzen in Japan. The couple was killed in the eruption.

Mount Unzen

MAURICE KRAFFT

BORN: March 25, 1946, Mulhouse, France

MARRIED: Catherine "Katia" Conrad, 1970

CHILDREN: None

DIED: June 3, 1991, Mount Unzen, Japan

CATHERINE "KATIA" (CONRAD) KRAFFT

BORN: April 17, 1942, Guebwiller, France

MARRIED: Maurice Krafft, 1970

CHILDREN: None

DIED: June 3, 1991, Mount Unzen, Japan

TONS OF TRAVEL

Studying volcanoes involves a lot of travel. Volcanoes are found all over the world. But most are in the Ring of Fire.

Volcanologists look at a volcano's shape. Some volcanoes have steep slopes. These have harmful eruptions. Others have gentle slopes. These have slow, smaller eruptions.

Volcanoes with gentle slopes are called shield volcanoes. The Hawaiian Islands are made up of shield volcanoes.

The Ring of Fire is a horseshoe-shaped area. It surrounds the Pacific Ocean. About 75 percent of Earth's volcanoes are found here.

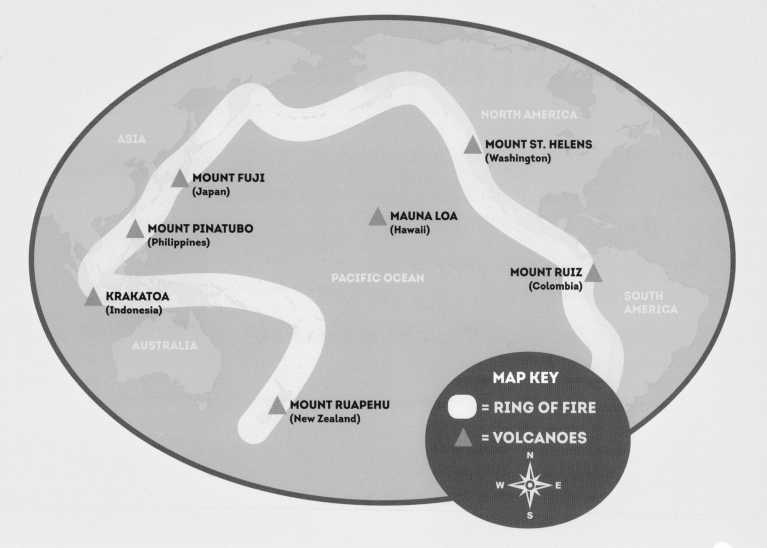

ASIA

NORTH AMERICA

MOUNT ST. HELENS
(Washington)

MOUNT FUJI
(Japan)

MAUNA LOA
(Hawaii)

MOUNT PINATUBO
(Philippines)

PACIFIC OCEAN

MOUNT RUIZ
(Colombia)

KRAKATOA
(Indonesia)

SOUTH AMERICA

AUSTRALIA

MOUNT RUAPEHU
(New Zealand)

MAP KEY

= RING OF FIRE

▲ = VOLCANOES

N
W   E
S

MANY MEASUREMENTS

Volcanologists learn about a volcano's eruption history. They collect rock and **lava** samples. They take measurements.

One measurement is **seismic** activity. Earthquakes can mean a volcano will erupt soon. Another measurement is temperature. Hot spots suggest **magma** is closer to the surface. Scientists also study a volcano's shape. Some volcanoes bulge before erupting. Others crack.

Mount St. Helens before its 1980 eruption (top) and today (bottom)

A bulge formed in Washington's Mount St. Helens in 1980. The volcano erupted soon after. This was the deadliest eruption in US history. Today, a new bulge is growing in the volcano's crater.

A VOLCANOLOGIST'S TOOL KIT

THERMAL IMAGING CAMERA
This takes **infrared** pictures. These pictures show the temperatures of volcanoes.

TILTMETER
This tool measures vertical ground movement. This is how much the ground rises or falls.

Volcanologists use tools to take measurements and stay safe.

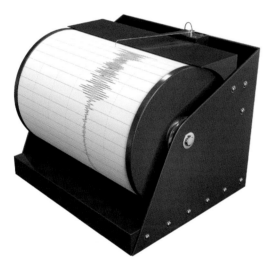

SEISMOGRAPH
This tool measures ground **vibration**. It can detect earthquakes.

HEAT-RESISTANT SUIT
This is a full-body suit. It protects the body from heat and fire. But it can be hard to move in!

THE NEXT ERUPTION?

Volcanologists make **predictions** carefully. A false prediction is harmful. People may not **evacuate** next time. But **technology** keeps improving.

National Aeronautics and Space Administration's (NASA's) VolcanoBot 1

Webcams help scientists watch volcanoes. **3-D** printers create 3-D maps of volcanoes. Scientists are building new robots. These can explore inside volcanoes. Predictions are getting better all the time!

BECOME A VOLCANOLOGIST!

Do you dream of becoming a volcanologist? Here are some things you can do now!

TAKE SCIENCE AND MATH CLASSES. Studying volcanoes involves math and science. Getting good grades in those classes now will help you in the future.

PRACTICE YOUR WRITING AND SPEAKING SKILLS. Volcanologists write a lot of papers. They give presentations about their research.

ASK QUESTIONS! Scientists ask a lot of questions. They look for new ways to find answers. You can get started now!

TEST YOUR KNOWLEDGE

1. Scientists who study volcanoes are called meteorologists.
   TRUE OR FALSE?

2. What year did Mount Vesuvius erupt?

3. In what area are most of Earth's volcanoes found?

THINK ABOUT IT!

What is the closest volcano to you? When was the last time it erupted?

ANSWERS: 1. False 2. Year 79 3. Ring of Fire

GLOSSARY

damage – harm or ruin.

evacuate – to leave or be removed from a place, especially for protection.

infrared – related to a type of light that people can't see.

lava – hot, melted rock from inside a volcano.

magma – melted rock below Earth's surface.

molten – melted by heat.

predict – to guess something ahead of time on the basis of observation, experience, or reasoning. This guess is called a prediction.

seismic – of or relating to vibrations in the earth.

technology – a capability given by the practical application of knowledge.

3-D – having length, width, and height and taking up space.

vibration – very small, quick movements back and forth.

webcam – a camera that is used to show live images or video on the Internet.